Restoring Women to Ceremony:
The Red Tent Resource Kit

Molly Remer

2015

Brigid's Grove

www.brigidsgrove.com

Restoring Women to Ceremony:
The Red Tent Resource Kit

© copyright 2015

Molly Remer, MSW, M.Div

First Edition 2015

ISBN-13:

978-1511459389

ISBN-10:

1511459387

Cover design and layout by Mark Remer

Hands photo on cover and photos on pages 7, 15, 63, and 72 by Karen Orozco.
All other photos by the author.

Brigid's Grove

www.brigidsgrove.com

"Do you feel it? The thrum of eternal wisdom galloping through your blood, the ancient and steady song that your bones sing quietly to you all night? Do you yearn to know the Mystery?"
-- Awakening Avalon

Contents

What is a Red Tent 7

Circle Basics 11

Purpose of Ritual 14

Elements of Ceremony & Raising Energy 15

Moontime Musings 19

Red Tent Recipes 25

Additional Resources 41

Poems & Readings 44

Womanprayers 48

Womanrunes in the Red Tent 52

Quotes for Discussion and Exploration 57

Womenergy 63

Resources/References 65

How to Make a Calamoondala 66

About the author 72

Gathering the Women

*Gathering the women
gathering the women
gathering the women.*

*You are welcome here.
You are welcome here.*

*Come join the circle
come join the circle
come join the circle.*

*You are welcome here.
You are welcome here.*

As I prepared an altar for a ritual one afternoon, I found myself singing this spontaneous song about gathering the women. This is what we do with Red Tent work: *gather the women*. We want them to feel welcome in the circle.

What is a Red Tent?

Red Tents are safe spaces for all women that transcend religious, cultural, and political barriers and are about coming together in sacred space as women. Red Tents honor and celebrate the "womanspirit" present within all of us. To paraphrase Deanna L'am, a Red Tent is a time and space devoted to connecting with each other as cyclical beings and speaking and listening from the heart about being women. We gather in Red Tent Circles for nurturing, self-care, connection, and sisterhood. Within the safety and sacredness of the Red Tent, women's experiences across the reproductive spectrum are "held" and acknowledged, whatever those experiences might be. Red Tent circles are intended for adult women of all ages, with nursing babies and daughters who have begun their menses also welcomed. Red Tent Circles need not focus exclusively on menstruation or on currently menstruating women, since all phases of a self-identified woman's life cycle and her many diverse experiences and feelings are held in the safe space of the circle. One of the core purposes in circling together is in *celebration*. We gather together each month to *celebrate* being women in this time and in this place, *together*.

Red Tent Circles may be held in a variety of settings, including living rooms, and usually feature red fabric draped in the room or other décor with a red theme.

The Red Tent Movement has roots in the women's spirituality and consciousness-raising movements of the 1970's. In 1997, Anita Diamant wrote a novel titled The Red Tent, which was a re-imagining of the Biblical story of Dinah. She drew inspiration for her story from the presence of moon lodges and menstrual huts in tribal and ancient cultures around the world as well as from historical evidence of Goddess worship. Diamant's novel was immensely captivating to many women and from it the contemporary Red Tent Temple Movement was born. Leaders in this movement include Alisa Starkweather, Deanna L'am, and Isadora Leidenfrost.

Once during a meeting for breastfeeding women, I mentioned wanting to start a group called "mothercraft" or "womancraft." Another woman there said it sounded interesting, but if that is what it was called she would *never come*. I surmised because it sounded too much like "witchcraft." I think many women retain a deep-seated, historically rooted fear of being labeled witches. Maybe that sounds silly, but this fear is a real one.

When I plan Red Tent events, though I do use Goddess imagery and I am Goddess-oriented in my personal spirituality, I do not usually include the word "Goddess" in the chants or rituals, because I want to make sure to speak to the womanspirit within all of us, rather than being associated with any one framework of belief. Red Tent spaces have the ability to transcend any particular belief system and welcome women of many backgrounds, inclinations, and beliefs. They aren't specifically "Goddess circles," though they honor the divine feminine through their very existence

I have also heard women remark that they don't need women's circles because they don't feel "oppressed." I haven't ever felt particularly oppressed personally, but I still *need* womancraft for *celebration* AND because even though I haven't been directly oppressed, that doesn't mean countless women around the world are not—I take a stand and lend a voice in my work for a different, healthier world for women. I've noticed many women seem to have significant difficulty in viewing women's circle activities as something other than an indulgence or something frivolous and so it is easy for them to talk themselves out of attending or not be able to give themselves the time or space for it, even though they are deeply intrigued and interested.

> *"[For centuries women have] had to withdraw their power – withdraw their energetic movement and flow. It had to be protected and hidden as the chalice of the woman had to survive.*
>
> *Now it is time for all to bring out their chalice – to gather their 'tribe' – to radiate their energetic flow. Now it is time to find the 'especial genius' that is intuitively woman. It is time for women to openly exhibit their power, their knowledge, and their leadership. The ancient symbol of unity is the circle. It is the sacred hoop of wholeness and female power. It represents the feminine spirit in a sacred space that is unbreakable. It is time to bring the circle – the hoop – to its power.*
>
> *It is time to restore the balance of the energies. For this to happen, you must first restore your own power – restore your own energies so that the balance of the humanity 'tribe' can be restored and all be lifted in the eternal flame of love. It is time to celebrate all of woman, in all of her beauty."*
>
> *Via Carla Goddard Sometimes You Have to Create The Thing You Want to Be Part Of – A Contemporary Perspective. (reprinted with permission)*

When we create intentional rituals they are, in themselves, a kind of "mandala of the whole universe." The ritual is like a miniature version, a microcosm, of a pattern which we would like to see expressed at a larger level. In the anthology, *Stepping Into Ourselves,* D'vorah Grenn writes about Jewish priestesses explaining, "… Every day, we witness the positive, transformative effects of, '**restoring women to ceremony**'…another reason it is vital that we continue our work…" (p. 56).

In 2008, a small postcard at the local Unitarian Universalist church caught my eye. It was for a *Cakes for the Queen of Heaven* facilitator training at Eliot Chapel in St. Louis. I registered for the training and went, driving alone into an unknown neighborhood. There, I circled in ceremony and sisterhood with women I'd never met, exploring an area that was new for me, and yet that felt so right and so familiar. I'd left my two young sons home for the day with my husband and it was the first time in what felt like a long time that I'd been on my own, as a *woman* and not someone's mother. At the end of the day, each of us draped in beautiful fabric and sitting in a circle around a lovely altar covered with goddess art and symbols of personal empowerment, I looked around at the circle of women and I *knew*: THIS is what else there is for me.

My work following the birth of my first son came to center heavily around pregnancy, birthing, and breastfeeding, the stage of life in which I was currently immersed. I'd wondered several times what I would do when those issues no longer formed the core of my interest and personal experience. How could I ever stop working with pregnant and birthing women? How could I stop experiencing the vibrance and power of pregnancy and birth? Would I become irrelevant in this field as my own childbearing years passed me by? Looking around the room at Eliot at *this* circle of women, only two of whom were also of childbearing age, I knew: my future purpose would be to hold circles like this one.

I found something in *Cakes* that I needed, the recognition that I wanted to celebrate and honor the *totality* of the female life cycle, not just pregnancy. As a girl, I loved the mother blessing ceremonies my mom and her friends held to honor each other during pregnancy. They hosted a coming of age blessingway for all of their early-teen daughters as well and I helped to plan a subsequent maiden ceremony for my younger sister several years later. Locally, we carried that tradition forward into the current generation of young mothers, holding mother blessings for each other and enjoying the time to celebrate and share authentically and deeply.

One of my stated purposes in holding monthly Red Tents in my own community is to honor and celebrate one another *without anyone needing to be pregnant*. Somehow, even though our own local mother blessing traditions were beautiful, we had accepted that the only time we had ceremonies with one another was when someone was pregnant.

Red Tent Circles bring a sense of celebration and power more fully into our lives as we honor the fullness and completeness of *women-in-themselves*, not just of value while pregnant or mothering.

At the center of my priestess altar, I placed a pottery bowl I made during a women's retreat. It feels like a symbol of gathering the women and **restoring them to ceremony**. Inside of it, I placed a tiny hummingbird feather as a reminder that these circles and relationships are delicate, surprising, beautiful, and need to be treated with care.

Circle Basics

"A Women's Circle helps you to find the river of your life and supports you in surrendering to its current."

–Marian Woodman
(quoted in Chrysalis Woman Circle Leader manual)

portions of this section are excerpted from Ritual Recipe Kit:
www.etsy.com/listing/186931189/ritual-recipe-kit-for-womens-ceremonies

Thinking in Circles

Circle round
circle round and celebrate
circle round and sing
circle round and share stories
circle round and reach out a hand

Circle

no beginning
no end...

In my college classes, I often tell my students that in working with people, **we need to learn to think in circles, rather than in lines**. Circles are strong. Circles are steady. Circles hold the space, circles make a place for others. Circles can expand or contract as needed. Circles can be permeable and yet have strong boundaries. Linked arms in a circle can keep things out and show solidarity. Linked energy in a circle can transform the ordinary into sacred space. Hands at each other's backs, facing each other, eye level. Working together in a circle for a ritual, change is birthed, friendships are strengthened, and love is visible.

I've noticed an increasing amount of offerings for sacred circles and sacred temples and councils of women that are all online or virtual. The websites advertising such programs often have beautiful photos of firesides and dancing and I find myself thinking, *where is the REAL fire?* If we spend all of our time at computers enjoying virtual sisterhoods and looking at *pictures* of fires, where are our real opportunities to dance by the fire hand in hand? Sometimes it is geographic or logistical, but it can also be because online connections may feel cleaner and less messy or complicated than face-to-face connections. It reminds me of my experiences in creating rituals for my family. In the books it looks so easy and fun. In real life, babies have poopy diapers and my sons make fart jokes and my papers blow away and I speak in a snappy tone of voice and things take longer than I expect. It is same with women's circles. Online, we can look at pretty pictures of flower crowns and crystal grids and flower mandalas and daydream how wonderful it would be to have a *real* women's circle, but in real life people don't always like each other, we interrupt each other, we talk too much or not enough or about the "wrong" things. As the facilitator of a ceremony in real life, portions might lag, people laugh at the wrong times, guided meditations might bring up painful experiences, people stop listening to each other, or they might forget something they were asked to bring. I might lose my place, sing off-key, or get distracted when someone is sharing something important.

As a priestess for sacred circles of women, I have to engage in what is called a process of "self-facing" that can be uncomfortable and sometimes stressful—the looking at my own shadows and shortcomings and then *doing it anyway*. Because it matters. Because it is *real*. I'm not saying that online connections aren't real or valuable, they can be tremendously so. What I *am* saying is that there is simply no substitute for standing *hand in hand* with flesh and blood women in a sacred circle. (Even if someone makes a fart joke.) Our hands matter. Real hands. Reaching out to one another. Our fingers may be too long, too short, too wrinkly, too skinny, too fat. Our hands may be too cold or too sweaty. We may be too loud, too quiet, too anxious, too confident, too self-conscious, too distracted, too intense. But...we can *show up*. We can offer what we offer and give what we give. Our whole, actual selves. Separated from the screens and other shields. Touching each other's actual hands and offering actual hugs rather than (((hugs))).

When I plan a Red Tent Circle, I want it to be nurturing, and celebratory, and fun and contemplative... somehow all at once! Oh, and not alienate anyone. And, not have it be lightweight and chatty OR heavy and tearful. Serious, but not too serious. No pressure! I'm also *real*. And, in the end, that is what I have to offer. There is a vulnerability and risk there as well as a courage.

Here's my hand.

Passing the Rattle?

Women's circle guidelines often suggest passing the rattle (or talking stick) as a means of giving each woman the floor in turn and making sure she has a full opportunity to speak and be heard. No interruptions and no opinions or advice. While this can be extremely powerful, in practice, I've noticed that the admonishment not to interrupt can dampen some of the natural magic of a sacred gathering of women. Fearing being seen as "interrupting" or messing up the passing of the rattle, women will silence themselves even when they have something important to offer to each other. While it might not be popular to say, I think that by laying down ground rules about no interrupting or advice-giving guideline within a circle, there is a very real chance in missing out on some of the dynamic, energetic, *living* fibers of connection that emerges in a safe circle for women. What if the very thing the woman with the rattle most needs in that moment is held within one of the other women in the circle, yet she withholds her magic out of fear of interrupting? What do we lose by silencing our own contributions and voices at the very moment we are trying to avoid silencing anyone? Since another element of health group work is "say what you need," in the circles with which I work, our guideline is *not* not to speak when someone else is talking, but rather to *ask for what you need* when you have the rattle—feedback and co-sharing or receptive witness. She gets to choose!

A powerful way to indicate that she is finished speaking is for each woman to state "**I have spoken**," after her turn with the rattle. This technique is used during salt bowl ceremonies taught by the Sacred Living Movement and it encourages women to take mindful ownership of their own voices.

Purpose of Ritual

> *"Genuine, heartfelt ritual helps us reconnect with power and vision as well as with the sadness and pain of the human condition. When the power and vision come together, there's some sense of doing things properly for their own sake."*
> —Pema Chodron in The Thundering Years: Rituals and Sacred Wisdom for Teens

> *"You will be teachers for each other. You will come together in circles and speak your truth to each other. The time has come for women to accept their spiritual responsibility for the planet"*
> —Sherry Anderson & Patricia Hopkins, The Feminine Face of God

Rituals are very important in acknowledging life passages—they say: *we care, we notice, we honor, we celebrate*. They mark transitions, celebrate accomplishments, and acknowledge losses. They provide a container for emotions, the opportunity to strengthen relationships and share experiences. They add meaning, value, and purpose to the events of our unique lives. They communicate love and appreciation. Elizabeth Gilbert explains that:

> *We do spiritual ceremonies as human beings in order to create a safe resting place for our most complicated feelings of joy or trauma, so that we don't have to haul those feelings around with us forever, weighing us down.*
>
> *We all need such places of ritual safekeeping.*
>
> *And I do believe that if your culture or tradition doesn't have the specific ritual you are craving, then you are absolutely permitted to make up a ceremony of your own devising, fixing your own broken-down emotional systems with all the do-it-yourself resourcefulness of a generous plumber/poet.*
>
> (Eat, Pray, Love)

Leading effective rituals involves awareness and management of the energetic balance and mood of a group while creating an effective container for change-work or self-discovery. Ritual facilitation also requires organization, planning, motivation, and self-confidence. It can be difficult, frustrating, overwhelming, and discouraging. It can also be exhilarating, rich, connected, and powerful.

Elements of Ceremony & Raising Energy

> *"I see a chain of women, each listening to each, being present to her as she waits for her Self to be born, for her feeling values to come to form and to birth... Woman after woman, being present, as each finds her voice"*
> —Judith Duerk: Journey to Herself

> *"The calling a woman feels to gather in Sacred Space with other Sisters starts first as a low and slow warmth that begins to burn. If left unfed, it rises quickly to a raging fire of desire. It will not be denied and can only be quenched by the nourishment of Truth, Candlelight, Song And Sisterhood"*
> —Ayla Mellani, Founder of Chrysalis Woman

In ritual practice with my own women's circle, since we are usually at a home, in a living room, it is necessary to create an atmosphere to "hold the space" and to signify our entrance into sacred circle, instead of everyday mundane life. The act of casting the circle is our signal, our sign, that we are now *doing something* and experiencing something together that is fundamentally different than hanging out with our kids at the park! We cast the circle in a very simple manner: we stand together in a circle and place our hands on each other's backs. Then, we hum in unison at least three times to pull our personal vibrations and rhythms into a sense of physical and literal harmony. After the group hum, we may smudge each other with sage to cleanse away any worries or concerns we may have brought with us and take turns reading an invocation to the four directions, lighting a candle, and reading an opening prayer. We consider the boundaries of our circle to be fairly fluid, encompassing the entire room in which we are in, including the bathroom. This is for practical purposes since our gatherings last about two hours or more and people do need some flexibility with entering and leaving the immediate circle. I do not find it necessary to symbolically draw the circle with any kind of object. I have a very body-based personal practice and find that our bodies and voices very effectively cast a circle without any need for additional objects.

Rituals need to be customized to time, purpose, occasion, theme, membership, and context. However, ritual does also involve some repetition, that is a part of what makes it powerful, and so the basic container can be similar, while the *working* portion and actual words used, then vary as needed. I've noticed in some books about ritual, or while participating in casually formatted rituals without a skilled priestess facilitating, that the *working* portion of a ritual may be overlooked. An effective ritual *must* accomplish something—there must a core of meaningful work built into the ritual.

Most rituals have:

Purpose—not rote, but meaningful, intentional, and planned for a specific reason, intention, or theme.

Structure--Invocation/circle casting, action, closing (opening of circle). This could also be viewed as the beginning, middle, and end to the ritual "story"/container. It is recognizable from the outside as "something happening."

Activity—these rituals are active processes, not passive with one person lecturing and others observing. They depend on engagement from participants.

Celebration/gratitude—these rituals do not typically involve supplication or requests, but celebrate the fact of being alive together in this space.

Theme—connection to natural world, celebration of our bodies, affirmation/acceptable of life change, etc.

Collaborative—not hierarchical. The members of the circles all share responsibility for the circle.

Notice that what is NOT included is any mention of a specific religion, deity, or should do list of what color of candle to include! Many people are starved for ritual, but they may also bear scars from religious rituals of their pasts. A song that we customarily sing during mother blessing ceremony–*Call Down Blessing*–has prompted the question, "blessings from where?!" During a body blessing ritual at a women's retreat, I was asked, "but WHO's doing the blessing?" As someone who does not personally come from a religious framework in which blessings are bestowed from outside sources–i.e. a priest/priestess or an Abrahamic God–the answer feels simple, *well, WE are*. We're blessing each other. When we "call down a blessing" we're invoking the connection of the women around us, the women of all past times and places, and of the beautiful world that surrounds us. We might each *personally add something more to that calling down*, but at the root, it is an affirmation of connection to the rhythms and cycles of relationship, time, and place. Blessings come from within and around us all the time, without requiring anything supernatural.

I believe that it is possible to plan and facilitate women's rituals that speak to the "womanspirit" in all of us and do not require a specifically shared spiritual framework or belief system in order to gain something special from the connection with other women.

In her book, The Power of Ritual, Rachel Pollack explains:

> *"Ritual opens a doorway in the invisible wall that seems to separate the spiritual and the physical. The formal quality of ritual allows us to move into the space between the worlds, experience what we need, and then step back and once more close the doorway so we can return to our lives enriched."*

She goes on to say:

> *"You do not actually have to accept the ideas of any single tradition, or even believe in*

divine forces at all, to take part in ritual. Ritual is a direct experience, not a doctrine. Though it will certainly help to suspend your disbelief for the time of the ritual, you could attend a group ritual, take part in the chanting and drumming, and find yourself transported to a sense of wonder at the simple beauty of it all without ever actually believing in any of the claims made or the Spirits invoked. You can also adapt rituals to your own beliefs. If evolution means more to you than a Creator, you could see ritual as a way to connect yourself to the life force..."

In *The Politics of Women's Spirituality,* writer Adrienne Rush observes, "the rituals being created today by various women are part of the renaissance of women's spirituality, that is, of the ultimate holiness or life-sacredness of women and the female creative process...this healing process is a vital one." She states, and I deeply agree, *"Women's spirituality groups can become birth centers for social change"* (p. 384).
I love this connection. I think people sometimes think of ritual as frivolous or just for fun or even silly, but these connections among women are of vital, transformative importance and of political significance as well.

> *"By prioritizing female-only space, whether in ritual or daily life, many women are able to find their center and explore their own truths. Baby girls are born through and into the unfolding mysteries of womanhood. The circle of womanhood is the very circle of life itself, for it is upon our sacred womb blood, the generative gift that is passed from mother to daughter, that human life depends. While all human beings celebrate this mystery, standing humbled by the enormity of it, only women can fully embody the experience."*
>
> --Ruth Barrett, *Women's Rites, Women's Mysteries: Intuitive Ritual Creation*

In *To Make and Make Again: Feminist Ritual Thealogy* by Charlotte Caron, we find many reminders that gathering with other women in a circle for ritual and ceremony is deeply important even though it might just *look* like people having fun. It is actually a microcosm of the macrocosm—a miniature version of the world we'd like to see and that we want to make possible. Caron explains: "Ritual change is symbolic change, but it can lead to direct action or to ideological change, so it can be an important element in strategizing for change. One way of causing change is to re-form or alter the system. This involves recognizing that we are part of the system and that the system is dependent on feedback from its parts to keep it in balance, which means that we have the capacity to change" (p. 209).

> *"Feminism catches fire when it draws upon its inherent spirituality. When it does not, it is just one more form of politics, and politics never fed our deepest hungers."*
>
> –Carol Lee Flinders (in *The Millionth Circle*)

> *"She walks not away from the fire...but toward it...because not only can she handle the HEAT... she contains it...and her fire wills forth the work that is meant to be in the world..."*
>
> --Anni Daulter

Moontime Musings

"...imagine what our lives would be like, what the world would be like if every womoon could bleed and birth inside a sacred circle..."

–Antiga in The Goddess Celebrates,

Cycle Wisdom

Blessing to our menstrual blood!
Blessing for our birthing blood!
Blessing to our female body
Blessing to our spirit
Blessing for our connection with other women
Blessing for our self-love and love of each other
Blessing to the world that holds us sacred.
–Antiga in The Goddess Celebrates, p. 168

> *"..by honouring the demands of our bleeding, our blood gives us something in return. The crazed bitch from irritation hell recedes. In her place arises a side of ourselves with whom we may not-at first- be comfortable. She is a vulnerable, highly perceptive genius who can ponder a given issue and take her world by storm. When we're quiet and bleeding, we stumble upon solutions to dilemmas that've been bugging us all month. Inspiration hits and moments of epiphany rumba 'cross de tundra of our senses..."*
> — Inga Muscio

I find an understanding of the emotional and creative cycle of the menstrual cycle immensely empowering. There is a natural outward directed phase of the cycle and there in an inward directed phase. In my own life, I try to be mindful of scheduling my commitments and my expectations for myself to coincide with the rhythms of my body. It took a long time for me to make the connection between birthing body wisdom and menstrual cycle wisdom….how do we honor this naturally "shamanic" time and inward connection in the midst of the swirl of daily life? What I'm finally figuring out is that there is a cycle of energy that goes with our moontime cycles and that life "flows" much more easily when I plan around those natural cycles of energy. For example, during ovulation I feel energetic, outward directed, focused, and creative. During this time, I compose new blog posts, work on articles, and do, do, do—and that feels good! Finally, I'm also realizing that I can *do stuff* during this energetic time in an advance *preparation* for the reduced energy and inward focus I feel during bleeding. I can take care of my future self, by focusing energy in powerful ways when I have it and then gathering in and being still when THAT is what I need instead. This is a new understanding for me, one that is still developing.

In the Moods of Motherhood, Lucy Pearce discusses this ebb and flow of energy as well, first with respect to children:

> This is a little discussed subject. I remember reading in The Wise Wound the fact that there was no research anywhere on the impact of women's cycles and PMS on children... and yet an effect there must be! We joke about women on the rag. Those around us suffer too, but we do not discuss it, or re-think family life at these times. They also see and feel the effects of our enhanced creativity, libido and need to retreat within. The whole family sails the seas of a mother's cycles…
>
> I am recognising in myself, my husband, and my kids the pressure valve, the thermostat which rises to boiling point, the markers that say: Please stop the overwhelm I CAN'T COPE. I am recognising that this is essential for our happy, healthy family co-existence. It is not a

sign of weakness or manipulation. It is very real: it is how we function and who we are. Pretending it is not the case, getting angry that it is, blaming others for our feelings or trying to ignore it does not work. It is at the point of overwhelm our instincts emerge, the reptilian brain literally takes over the show – we lash out, scream, yell... now is not the time for moralising, for punishments, for anger... now is the time for de-compression...

Lucy goes on to explain:

I think the most important thing any person can do is to know themselves and try to find balance amongst the various strands of themselves. And for a woman to know her cycles and her energy levels and work to these rather than against herself. This is absolutely what I try to do. But most often I fail on the balance front – I do too much and then burn out. In our culture this is seen as a good thing... but really it's a form of ego driven insanity.

Many menstrual empowerment activists draw upon the idea of four seasons as a metaphor for understanding the energy of your cycle. The seasons idea helps create an enhanced place of understanding about your own ebb and flow of energy, enthusiasm, and creativity.

Winter is the first stage, when we bleed. Our moontime. Emotionally, it is a time of wanting to withdraw, hibernate, or cocoon. We may feel withdrawn, pull inward, and it can be difficult to focus or feel energetic. Our energy feels reserved, pulled into ourselves, versus gregarious and outer directed.

Spring is the week following our moontime and we may suddenly feel more energized, passionate, friendly, and outward-focused. We may be sociable and wish to spend time with others. We want to get stuff done quickly and do so with grace and ease.

Summer is the time of ovulation. Energetically we may feel as if we are bursting forth, blooming, expansive, and open. We reach our peak.

Autumn is when we start the inward journey or descent back into ourselves. We may experience what is known as PMS and feel snappy, tense, taut, and overwhelmed. The projects we took on and passionately pursued during spring and summer may suddenly feel like "too much" and we may cast our eyes around for things (or even people!) to trim from our lives and schedules.

What I find transformative about this understanding is the acceptance that comes from realizing what season I'm in and knowing that a new season is coming. Rather than get frustrated with myself during autumn or winter, thinking it means a permanent state of being, I recognize, "ah ha! This sense of needing to pull in and retreat. I know this. Time to break out some of those saved guided meditations, say no to things I can say no to, and sit down with a book and some tea." Before using the season metaphor, I would have taken this impulse as a sign that my life is too crowded and I MUST. QUIT. SOMETHING. NOW. THINGS. MUST CHANGE. ARGHHHH. NO MORE! Now, I see that it is just a call for *right now*, for this *little season*, not a **permanent** change, just an honoring of body rhythms.

However, it is also very, very easy for me to forget that many of the common mental patterns I experience with needing to retreat and wanting to quit and wanting to *rest* are cyclical in nature . I've never wanted "must be hormones!" to be an *excuse*. I honestly think it isn't an excuse though, but is instead a wake-up call. It surprises me how, even though I track my cycle using a handy phone app, I still overlook that the "I'm so fat and ugly!" thoughts and the "how come I suddenly have zits on my chin?" and "I want to QUIT

THE WORLD" and, "people are so annoying and SO LOUD and never STOP TALKING!!!!!" and, "WHY do people WANT things from me ALL THE TIME!!!!" feelings, also recur on a cyclical basis. And, then moontime comes, and suddenly life takes a turn for the better and things look up. I start feeling energetic and productive and excited about things. Instead of wanting to quit, I have tons of new ideas and feel enthusiastic and optimistic about completing them. I feel creative and inspired. If I am able to remember, "oh, *this*. This sensation of wanting to hide…I remember this," and this is the key…then DO IT. Go ahead and hide for a minute. Things will go on without me. It is when I override my own inclinations and body messages and needs that "Dragon Lady" comes out and roars for her rights.

> *"Each time we deny our female functions, each time we deviate from our bodies' natural path, we move father away from out feminine roots. Our female bodies need us now more than ever, and we too need the wisdom, the wildness, the passion, the joy, the vitality and the authenticity that we can gain through this most intimate of reconciliations."*
> –Sarah J Buckley, M.D.

> *"…Could it be that women who get wild with rage do so because they are deeply deprived of quiet and alone time, in which to recharge and renew themselves?*
> *Isn't PMS a wise mechanism designed to remind us of the deep need to withdraw from everyday demands to the serenity of our inner wilderness? Wouldn't it follow, then, that in the absence of quiet, sacred spaces to withdraw to while we bleed — women express their deprivation with wild or raging behaviors?…"*
> –DeAnna L'am via Occupy Menstruation

Indigo Bacal, in her online presentation Womb Magic, shares three things every cycling woman should know.

1. **track your cycle**
2. **create a moon tent and spend time in it** *alone*.
3. **moontime is a powerful opportunity for renewal**

One of the things she also shares is that if your family and the people around you can allow you the space to retreat into your "moon tent," you will return with *powerful medicine* for them every month, because of this powerful opportunity moontime offers us for **renewal**. It is the blocked call for quiet time to rest and renew that causes a variety of premenstrual tension, strain, and stress.

> *"The revolution must have dancing; women know this. The music will light our hearts with fire, The stories will bathe our dreams in honey and fill our bellies with stars…"*
> –Nina Simons in We'Moon 2012

> *"A woman's best medicine is quite simply herself, the powerful resources of her own deep consciousness, giving her deep awareness of her own physiology as it changes from day to day."*
> —Veronica Butler and Melanie Brown

While many TV ads would have you assume that it is physical symptoms that "interfere" with a woman's life during menstruation (i.e. cramps, bloating, etc.), I find it is actually the reverse—that normal life *interferes* with my body's call. As I've tuned in more fully to my body's moontime rhythms, I've realized that aside from the killer headache that heralds moontime's approach about two days prior, I don't really feel bad, sick, or particularly yucky during menstruation. It isn't at all that I don't feel well, it is that I feel like being **alone**, turning inward and away, withdrawing, and being creative. I feel like cocooning and feel easily disturbed or disrupted from that needed cocoon. It reminds me of the postpartum experience following a baby's birth and I explain to my husband that taking some time off from my regular roles to rest and *be* during moontime, truly makes as much senses as essential as doing so during postpartum. I try to remind mindful of the ebb and flow of my cycle and associated emotions, feelings, and inclinations. Just as I wouldn't expect myself to "do it all" during postpartum, I find it logical that I shouldn't expect myself to "do it all" during menstruation either. But, that is easier said than done! Kids still need to go to playgroup and taekwondo and, and, and...

I've also noticed emotional vulnerability to any criticism, increased irritability and impatience, and usually a monthly breakdown of some kind in which I generally decree that *something MUST change* ™, usually precipitating big life-revisions plans (maybe including charts/diagrams), long discussions, flawed self-analysis, harsh assessments, and endless ruminating along with self-recrimination. This is usually followed with an invigorating surge of energy, enthusiasm, and creativity on the actual first day of bleeding.

> *"When a woman begins her monthly bleeding, she has a very special vibration. The blood flow is cleansing as the old uterine lining is sloughed off, one monthly reproductive cycle ended. At menstruation, women have the chance to rid themselves of all old thoughts, habits, and desires, and be receptive to new visions and inspirations for the next cycle...*
>
> *If a woman continues her normal routine at menstruation, then she loses a uniquely female opportunity for introspection. She also finds she gets more tired, irritable, and upset because her physical rhythm has slowed down. She needs rest, more time for meditation, and less time doing housework, cooking, working in the outside world, and taking care of children."*
>
> —Marcia Starck, Women's Medicine Ways

"A woman who becomes aware of her cycle and inherent connection to the whole, also learns to perceive a level of life that goes beyond the visible; she maintains an intuitive link with the energies of life, birth and death, and feels the divinity within the Earth and herself. From this recognition woman deals not only with the visible and the earthly but with the invisible and spiritual aspects of her existence. It was through this altered state of consciousness that was taking place every month than the shamans/healers and priestesses, contributed to the world and to their own community its power, clarity and connection with the divine."

—Miranda Gray, Red Moon

"There is magic inherent in the menstrual cycle. Each cycle provides a woman with the opportunity to understand and read the messages her body gives her for any specific healing she needs. Each cycle creates the opportunity for as much spiritual growth and personal development that she could want. All a woman has to do to connect with that potential is simply to be with what is, her cycle, happening over and over."

—Jane Hardwicke Collings, "The Spiritual Practice of Menstruation"
(Check out her fabulous work www.moonsong.com.au)

Red Tent Recipes

We who bleed

we who pour libation to the earth each moon,

weave toward the sea.

These are the priestesses who carry me.

Each moon, each woman

nourishes this soil that suckles us.

We the bloodrich, we the generous.

–Sue Silvermarie in Open Mind

Red Tent Ritual Recipe

Here I am
this is me
I am woman
giving birth to myself...

Your Red Tent will look different each time you gather, but you can create the same general container each time using this recipe (and substituting different activities, as needed into the spaces for different months).

Allow about thirty minutes at the opening of the circle for women to arrive and settle in. They can make tea, choose a place to sit, do some coloring, drawing, or journaling. This transition time allows the women to soften into the space and energy of the circle rather than rushing to begin straight away.

1. Group hum—an element common to all women's rituals for which I priestess, we cast the circle with our own bodies by standing in a circle and placing our hands on each other's backs. Then, we hum together three times in order to unify our energy, to harmonize, to focus our intention and to bring our minds and bodies solidly into the ritual space. This simple, powerful action is a point of continuity from circle to circle that we all value.

> *Guidelines for an Enjoyable Group:*
>
> 1. Speak only for yourself--use "I" messages.
> 2. Share what is comfortable. Do not pressure others to share.
> 3. Feel free to pass.
> 4. Do not give advice.
> 5. Tell your own story.
> 6. Be openminded and nonjudgmental.
> 7. Wait until the person speaking has finished before you speak (pass the rattle as necessary)
> 8. Ask for what you need.
> 9. Hold the stories from the circle sacred and close to your heart (what is said in the circle, stays in the circle).
> 10. Avoid chit-chat and dig deep!

2. Group introductions and maternal line using red cord (based on Deanna L'am's Red Tent Host Manual, deannalam.com). This cord symbolizes our "mother line," the red thread of the generations stretching through time and space to the first woman who ever lived as well as forward into the future.

> Holding a ball of red satin cording, yarn, or ribbon, mindfully wrap the end around your left (heart's) wrist while you say your name, the names of your mother, grandmother, and the women of your mother's line as far back as you can, ending with Mother Earth. Continue by reciting the names of your daughters, stepdaughters, heart-daughters, or granddaughters, if you have them. For example: "I am Molly, daughter of Barbara, daughter of Lyla, daughter of Marjorie, daughter of Caroline, daughter of Katherine. daughter of Mother Earth. I am Molly, mother of Alaina."

3. Sing *May All Mothers Know*

> *May all mothers know that they are loved.*
> *May all sisters know that they are strong.*
> *May all daughters know that they are powerful.*
> *That the circle of women may live on.*
> *That the circle of women may live on.*
>
> Circle of Women | Nalini.

4. Pass rattle...and take turns with group discussion about our cycles and current relationship to (you may wish to discuss the "seasons" metaphor explored in the resource packet included with this kit). OR: Our Bodies Today--how does she feel and can you give her what she needs...

5. Lie down for *Elemental Connecting* visualization (included as separate handout) and journal about experiences.

6. Do *She* reading, in circle together (this is a poem for multiple voices. Go around the circle each reading a line. OR, have the circle facilitator read the bolded lines and the other women in the circle in turn respond with each subsequent line).

> *SHE...*
> **She who is open to possibilities.**
> She who has taken her own journey
> >carved her own path
> >learned her own lessons
> >and carries her own wisdom.
>
> **She who carries the story of a woman's life written on her body.**
> She who has spun cells into life
> She who has traveled
> >laughed
> >shared stories
> >danced
> >hugged
> >cried.
>
> **She who is...**
> >complete
> >magnificent
> >ever-changing
> >surprising
> >unmistakably
> >>**SHE...** [all say together]

7a. Song to close--*Woman Am I*.

> *Woman am I*
> *Spirit am I*
> *I am the infinite within my soul*
> *I have no beginning*
> *And I have no end*
> *All this I am*

7b. OR: *Dance in a Circle of Women*...with drumbeat to accompany and perhaps actual dancing!

> *Dance in a circle of women*
> *Make a web of my life*
> *Hold me as I spiral and spin*
> *Make a web of my life*
>
> *(Marie Summerwood)*

8. Make Happy Woman Tea or Intention Candles (recipes follow) or spend time at the art table, with your journal, or other self-care activities/stations you may have arranged (henna, etc.) You may wish to have a Red Tent playlist of music playing at this time. (See Appendix.)

9. Ask the women to bring a candle back each time and use as part of opening circle---each woman speaks her name, lights her candle, and adds it to the central altar.

10. Ask for volunteers for self-care activities/stations, bodywork, for future Red Tent Circles.

Note: You can listen to our local Red Tent Circle's version of many of the songs and readings in this book by going to our Red Tent Circle album on SoundCloud: https://soundcloud.com/brigidsgrove/sets/red-tent-circle

Intention Candle Recipe

Tall candle in glass holder
Magazines, cards, poems, stickers
Beads or charms
Ribbon, cord, string, or yarn
Glue

Cut out images and words and collage the glass outside of the candle. String beads or charms on ribbon or cord (perhaps from the "mother line" beginning part of the ceremony) and tie around to the top of the candle.

A combination of a vision board and an altar candle, with each lighting of your intention candle throughout the year your most powerful conscious intentions and commitments are reinforced, reaffirmed, and strengthened.

Happy Woman Tea Recipe

(modified from the Sacred Postpartum course from the Sacred Living Movement)

Alfalfa – 2 cups
Motherwort – 2 cups
Red raspberry leaf – 2 cups
Nettle – 2 cups
Cinnamon – 1 cup

Mix dry herbs together in a mixing bowl. Stir gently because the cinnamon will puff! (Make sure not to breathe it in.) Divide into glass jars or plastic bags. To use, steep approximately two teaspoons of the mix (using a tea ball) in hot water for about five minutes (longer steeping may increase bitter taste).

This loose tea blend is perfect for making and enjoying together in the Red Tent. Many women find that drinking this tea replenishes something in them that they need. The herbs used are said to help with hormonal balancing, anxiety and stress reduction, calming, and immune system support. You can buy the herbs in bulk from Frontier Herbs.

(*Due to the uterine stimulant properties of some of the ingredients in this tea, depending on her history [any losses or pre-term labor] pregnant women may wish to wait to enjoy it until they are close to full term.)

Elemental Connecting ... A Meditation

Feel the bones of your body, feel their strength and solidity.
Feel the stones of the earth, feel their strength and solidity.
The stones of the earth and the bones of your body are one in mineral foundation, they are one in strength and support.
Feel your bones connecting with the stones.
Feel your solidity and stability.

Feel the waters of your body in your cells and tissues, feel their flow and movement.
Feel the waters of the earth, streams rushing, rivers flowing, seas pulsing.
The waters of the earth and the waters of your body are one in dynamic flow and movement, they are shared by all beings.
Feel the waters of your cells connecting with the waters of the earth.
Feel your fluidity and depth.

Feel the air in your body, expanding your lungs, infusing your cells and blood. Feel the air of the earth, softly caressing your face, gusting trees into dance, moving dunes into new landforms.
They are one in expansiveness and dance.
Feel the air of your body connecting with the air of the earth.
Feel your movement and freedom.

Feel the fire in your body, the heat of cellular change and growth.
Feel the fire of the earth, sun hot on your skin, hot springs steaming to the surface, lava flowing new earth into being.
They are one in transformative potential and creative force.
Feel the fire in your body connecting with the fire of the earth.
Feel your passion and vibrance.

Breathe and feel the elements meeting in your body.
Breathe again...
Breathe and feel yourself intimately connected to the earth.
Breathe some more...

Reprinted with permission — tracienichols.com — © 2011 Tracie Nichols - All Rights Reserved

Red Tent Ritual Recipe II

1. **Group hum (stand with hands on each other's backs, hum three times)**

2. Intro and maternal line with red thread

   > Holding a big ball of crimson cord, mindfully wrap the end around your left (heart's) wrist a few times while you speak your name, the names of your mother, grandmother, and the women of your mother's line as far back as you can, ending with Mother Earth. Continue by reciting the names of your daughters, stepdaughters, heart-daughters, or granddaughters, if you have them. For example: "I am Molly, daughter of Barbara, daughter of Lyla, daughter of Marjorie, daughter of Caroline, daughter of Katherine. daughter of Mother Earth. I am Molly, mother of Alaina."

3. **The River She is Flowing song**

   > *The river she is flowing, flowing and growing*
   > *The river she is flowing, down to the sea*
   > *Mother carry me, your child I'll always be*
   > *Mother carry me, down to the sea*

4. Pass rattle...discussion with:

   > "The revolution must have dancing; women know this. The music will light our hearts with fire, The stories will bathe our dreams in honey and fill our bellies with stars..." –Nina Simons in We'Moon 2012
   >
   > **What is your revolution?**
   >
   > "A woman's best medicine is quite simply herself, the powerful resources of her own deep consciousness, giving her deep awareness of her own physiology as it changes from day to day." –Veronica Butler and Melanie Brown
   >
   > **What is your medicine?**

5. Divination cards: use Womanrunes or another divination system like the Mother's Wisdom deck. Each woman should choose a card and then drape a scarf over her head. Dim the lights and play a song such as Grandmother by Nina Lee (available via iTunes on the Sacred Pregnancy The Deep Drink album). After the song is complete, journal about or draw the messages first and then read about the interpretation.

6. Dance—wearing jingly hip scarves or other adornments, dance, drum, and sing together!

> *Dance in a circle of women*
> *Make a web of my life*
> *Hold me as I spiral and spin*
> *Make a web of my life*
>
> *(Marie Summerwood)*

7. Make Moon Pendants—bring crescent moon charms or other beads and charms and create moon pendants to wear to future circles (or as a signal to one's family that you're on your moon time)

8. Hold hands and sing **Woman am I** (page 28).

Red Tent Ritual Recipe III

1. **Group hum (stand with hands on each other's backs, hum three times)**

2. Intro and maternal line with red thread

   > Holding a big ball of crimson cord, mindfully wrap the end around your left (heart's) wrist a few times while you speak your name, the names of your mother, grandmother, and the women of your mother's line as far back as you can, ending with Mother Earth. Continue by reciting the names of your daughters, stepdaughters, heart-daughters, or granddaughters, if you have them. For example: "I am Molly, daughter of Barbara, daughter of Lyla, daughter of Marjorie, daughter of Caroline, daughter of Katherine. daughter of Mother Earth. I am Molly, mother of Alaina."

3. May all mothers know song (page 27).

4. Pass rattle...discussion with *Moon Time* quote:

   > "It is my guess that no one ever initiated you into the path of womanhood. Instead, just like me, you were left to find out by yourself. Little by little you pieced a working understanding of your body and soul together. But still you have gaps." —Lucy Pearce
   >
   > Questions for circle: Were you initiated into the "path of womanhood"? What gaps do you feel?

5. Moon Yoga practice (see page 38 for script).

6. **I Honour You** group reading (page 37 each woman reads one stanza aloud)

7. Song to close--**Woman am I** (page 28).

Red Tent Ritual Recipe IV

1. **Group hum (stand with hands on each other's backs, hum three times)**

2. State your name and do a physical check-in (We may be used to spending a lot of time in our heads. Today, we will use our bodies to check in. As we go around the circle, communicate with your body rather than words how you feel right now.)

3. Body Prayer from the book *Wild Girls* by Patricia Mongahan.

   > 1. Hands on your heart, take a couple of centering breaths.
   > 2. Raise your open arms to the sky with face looking up.
   > 3. Bring your hands back to your heart.
   > 4. Touch the ground below you.
   > 5. Standing up, put your hands back on your heart
   > 6. Slowly, with left hand on heart and right arm outstretched, face looking to the right, begin to turn your body in a full circle.
   > 7. Repeat with opposite hand.
   >
   > *Welcome to the circle! We're so glad you're here!*

4. Sing **May all Mothers Know** song (page 27).

5. Living the Questions journal exercise based on *Comfort Secrets for Busy Women* by Jennifer Louden (free write first response to each):

   - What do you most need in your life right now?
   - Choose one thing that you most need (ask your heart!). What is one specific, achievable thing you can do to bring more of _____ into your life?
   - What do you need less of in your life right now?
   - Choose one thing (ask your heart!) and ask yourself what is one specific, achievable thing you can do to reduce the presence of _____ in your life.
   - Make yourself a "not to do" list with one thing on it and commit to *not doing* that thing in the upcoming week or month.

6. Pass the rattle to check in with journal responses. Draw a Womanrunes card if desired as a message or guidance for the coming month.

7. Sing Call Down a Blessing (each woman chooses a word to insert as the song moves around the circle).

8. *Call down a blessing*

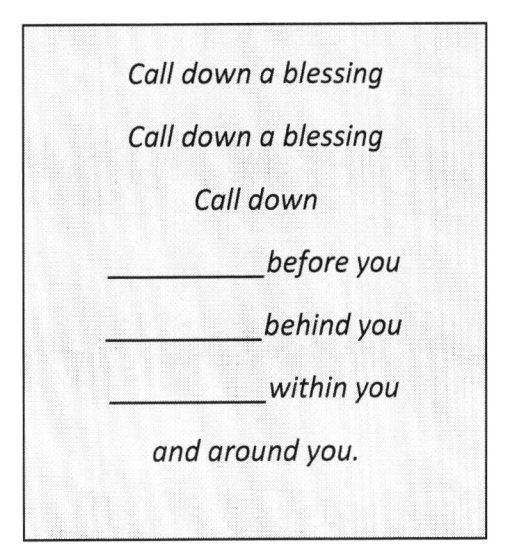

> Call down a blessing
>
> Call down a blessing
>
> Call down
>
> _____ before you
>
> _____ behind you
>
> _____ within you
>
> and around you.

9. **I Honour You poem** (page 37)

10. Song to close--**Woman am I** (page 28).

Simple Red Tent Ongoing Ritual Recipe

- Have tea and possibly other refreshments

- Each woman brings candle to light, or sacred symbol to add to central altar

- Group hum

- May All Mothers Know Song

- Pass the rattle and/or topical discussion

- Meditation/Journal

- Self-care/nurturing activity

- Woman Am I or Dance in a Circle of Women song

- Have art table available and divination/inner guidance corner available for spontaneous use.

Shakti Woman Speaks

Shakti woman speaks
She says Dance
Write
Create
Share
Speak.

Don't let me down
I wait within
coiled at the base of your spine
draped around your hips
like a bellydancer's sash
snaking my way up
through your belly
and your throat
until I burst forth
in radiant power
that shall not be denied.

Do not silence me
do not coil my energy back inside
stuffing it down
where it might wither in darkness
biding its time
becoming something that waits
to strike.

Let me sing
let me flood through your body
in ripples of ecstasy
stretch your hands wide
wear jewels on your fingers
and your heart on your sleeve

Spin
spin with me now
until we dance shadows into art
hope into being
and pain into power.

I Honour You

In circle gathered
In circle blessed
In circle joined
In circle One

She who weaves and writes and dances and draws
Creative Woman I honour you

She who looks herself in the mirror of her soul
Honest Woman I honour you

She who looks fear in the face, embraces it and laughs
Brave Woman I honour you

She who stands at the gateway of the worlds and holds the key for those who would explore
Holy Woman I honour you

She who soothes the salt of tears
with the sweat of her brow
Compassionate Woman I honour you

She who sees the pot of gold
in the rainbow's brilliant arc
Visionary Woman I honour you

She whose hands labour to prepare the fertile ground,
to plant, water, weed and gather the fruit
Abundant Woman I honour you

She who listens and looks and learns
Thinking Woman I honour you

She who greets the dawn of the day
in all her beauty unclothed
Free Woman I honour you

She who births and bleeds,
nurtures and knows,
loves and laughs,
dances and dreams,
sobs and smiles,
stumbles and stands,
gives and is grateful,
and follows her path through life with heart

All together: Sister I Honour You

by Helen Ramoutsaki
Shared at International Women's Conference with this message:
this poem is a gift to all women, you are welcome to copy it and pass it on to other women.

Moon Yoga

- Starting with **pelvic circles**, tip your pelvis forward and then roll onto your right hip, around to your left hip and continuing circling as you take slow, easy breaths. You can make large circles, your shoulders moving softly along for the ride, or make smaller circles. Make sure to go in both directions so each side of your body gets a gentle massage.

    Pelvic circles help you relax your body, your mind, and help you find a sense of balance and focus.

- From pelvic circles, gently come onto your hands and knees into **cat/cow position** another very supportive position.

- Gently tilt the pelvis, rocking, opening the heart with slow, easy breaths. Cat/cow can relieve back tension or help you stretch out any parts of your body that may be tightened up.

- Breathe and let yourself rock through all these spaces, using your intuition to help you see what feels best for you in this time, in this space.

- From **cat/cow, open your legs wide**, sinking your hips down very low and make large, circular motions with the hips. Breathe, to help you release tension and anxiety. Again, circle in both directions, doing what feels most appropriate at this time.

- Sink down into **supported child's pose**. It can be a very relaxing and restorative pose.

- Really let yourself release, creating space in your body. Breathe and just relax.

- **Moonflowers**: come up to standing with legs wide apart, dip your knees into a wide squat and bring your arms down low as if you are scooping up flowers. Sweep your arms up overhead as you straighten your les (still wide apart) and curve your arms as if you are cradling a wide, full moon. Repeat about six times—scooping down to gather flowers, stretching up to embrace the moon. End with **Goddess pose:** legs in a wide squat and hand sin prayer position in front of your chest. **Open and release. Flow and let go.**

- Sink down again into **supported child's pose**. It can be a very relaxing and restorative pose.

- **End with Savasana (lying flat on yoga mat) and brief relaxation meditation:** Feel your body becoming soft and heavy. Melting down into the support that surrounds you. Feeling the surface you are on, completely holding and cradling you. And know that beneath this support is the support of Mother Earth, the planet below you. Cradling you firmly, while spinning through space in the same moment. Feel the weight of your body. Let it sink. Let it be held, supported, enfolded, nurtured, cherished, and nourished. Take three long, deep, slow breaths...

    Begin to feel your toes and feet soften and relax. Then, let that wave of relaxation, that quiet, soothing energy, let it spread. Up through your calves, knees, thighs. Let the relaxation sweep through your pelvis, hips, belly. Let the relaxation travel through your ribcage, your chest, your shoulders. Let them soften and pull away, dropping down away from your ears, releasing any tightness or tension you might be holding there. And then let the relaxation travel down your arms, into your hands, softening and spreading your fingers, feeling them rest loose and easy, totally at ease, totally relaxed, totally supported. And, with the next breath let your face soften and smooth. Feel your neck rest easy and loose. The skin on your forehead softens and smooths. Your eyebrows soften and release. Your eyes relax and sink down. Teeth unclench. Lips part. Soft and smooth. Easy.

- Breathe.
- When you feel ready, wiggle your fingers and toes, open your eyes, and come back into the room.
- *Namaste.*

Adapted from a series of poses in Yoga for Your Pregnancy DVD by Lamaze (Lamaze.org).

Additional Resources

"It is now time for all women of the colorful mind, who are aware of the cycles of night and day and the dance of the moon in her tides, to arise."

–Dhyani Ywahoo (in Open Mind)

Additional Project Ideas

- Foot baths (can be combined with salt bowl ceremony)—each woman brings her own bowl or container large enough for her own feet as well as an offering of herbs, oils, flowers, or salts to contribute to the group. Each woman selects her own customized blend and adds it to her bath. Sitting in a circle, women enjoy the nurturing of soaking their feet together in communal sisterhood. Afterward, women can massage lotion onto their own feet or, depending on comfort level, in circle format, each woman can apply lotion to the woman next to her (each woman puts a foot on the lap of the sister next to her until all women in the circle have a foot in one woman's lap being massaged, while they are massaging the foot of a woman in their own lap).
- Yoga—a group moon or sun salutation works well
- Vision board collage—works well at beginning of year.
- Choose a pretty card and write a note to yourself—a note of encouragement or support, a reminder or an apology. Seal into self-addressed, stamped envelopes. Give all sealed cards to facilitator who then mails them back at a future date (chosen intuitively).
- Henna
- Inner Wisdom Meditation—choose card from a divination, oracle, or guidance deck. Contemplate intuitive understanding without looking up interpretation. Dim lights, drape scarf over head and listen to song (such as Grandmother by Nina Lee, available via iTunes, or another song from the suggested playlist) while meditating on chosen card. At song's close, journal about the card, experiences, and draw it or the messages you received. Finally, read interpretation and do any additional journaling.
- Miranda Gray's Womb Blessing (wombblessing.com/)
- Guided visualization or meditation
- Shamanic journeying drum CD
- Draw mandalas or do mandala coloring pages.
- Make moon necklaces (supply kit available from Brigid's Grove: brigidsgrove.etsy.com)
- Healing touch: share massage, reiki, bodywork, or other healing modalities
- Salt bowl ceremony—each woman brings an item representing her purest intention to contribute to a collective salt bowl. The bowl of sea salt is in the center of the room. In turn, each woman approaches the bowl, offers her intention and adds her offering to the bowl. After she has spoken her intention she says, "I Have Spoken" and the next woman approaches the bowl. After each woman has participated in the ceremony, the salt can be divided into individual containers for the women to take home (later using the salt for a ceremonial bath when she needs a powerful boost of intention in her life) or some of the salts can be used for foot baths as described above.
- Fire of transformation ceremony—write down all the negative messages you've received about menstruation and/or your body on slips of paper. Then transform them by burning the papers in a fireproof container. You may wish to read the messages aloud before casting them into the flames, announcing, "I release…" each message as it is transformed through fire.
- Calamoondala (see additional handout to follow)
- Create SoulCollage or personal oracle cards (use magazines to collage individual personal oracle cards

based on various themes such as Self-Care, Inner Strength, Power, The Warrior, The Child Self, Wisdom, etc.) See soulcollage.com/.
- Divination using Womanrunes, a pendulum, or other oracle systems such as The Gaian Tarot, Soul Clarity Cards, The Mother's Wisdom Deck and many more.
- Scarf dance (See example: https://youtu.be/a_qw87rJghI)

Note: You can listen to our local Red Tent Circle's version of many of the songs and readings in this book by going to our Red Tent Circle album on SoundCloud: https://soundcloud.com/brigidsgrove/sets/red-tent-circle

Playlist:

We Are Circling	Nina Lee	Sacred Pregnancy — The Deep Drink
Standing at the Edge	Nina Lee	Sacred Pregnancy — The Deep Drink
Full Height of Our Power	Kellianna	Elemental
Woman Am I, Blessed Am I	Alice D Micele	Circle of Women
Ebb and Flow	Kellianna	Elemental
Sacredness (The Blood Song)	Shylah Ray Sunshine	Earth Medicine Music
Daughters of the Earth	Kellianna	The Ancient Ones
Grandmother	Nina Lee	Sacred Pregnancy — The Deep Drink
Direction Song	Kelliana	Elemental
Gentle with Myself	Karen Drucker	Songs of the Spirit III

Potpourri technique for women's ceremonies:

After several years of planning and priestessing women's circles on my own, I introduced what I call the "potpourri" technique. Instead of the circle leader or facilitator planning the entire ritual, ask each participant to bring something to share. It can be a poem, a reading, a project, a craft, a meditation, or an activity. You create the basic container for the ritual—i.e. opening, closing, and perhaps a meditation or short project—and the other women fill in the middle with the contributions they have brought. This technique allows each woman an opportunity to contribute her unique gifts to the circle and it relieves the pressure the facilitator may feel in being responsible for the process of every circle and ceremony. While I find it is very important for the longevity of the circle to have a skillful, committed "center-holder" in the form of one or two primary group facilitators, the health and functioning of the circle also rests with the participants—those who *show up* to do this work together. Each member of the circle shares responsibility for the functioning, health, and enjoyability of any circle. The identified leader does not hold all the power in what works or doesn't work in the circle environment, it is a *shared* responsibility and a shared process of co-experiencing, co-creation, and mutual unfolding.

Restoring Women to Ceremony: The Red Tent Resource Kit

Poems and Readings

Prayer to and from the Mother

The purpose of the invocation is to ground us in our bodies, while also connecting us to the larger swirl of energies that surround us. As I composed it, I envisioned a circle, in which we are embedded and moving within. This invocation itself then creates a *circle* and brings the immanent and transcendent *together* into shared space, as it both invokes the elements and awakens your body.

The words included in parentheses are optional replacements or additions, according to your specific group's needs.

Feet planted solidly on Mother Earth
Drawing up
Solid
Gaia energy
Rich life
Pulsing planet
Power of being

Shoulders back
Chest open
Breathe in the Breath of Life
Wind
Air
Oxygen
Swirling
Flowing
Breathing you
Spreading your arms
Hands open
Feel the pulse of your heart
Blood flowing
Life giving
Throughout your body
The blood of your womb (veins)
Matching the tides of the ocean
And the pull of the moon
Linked in watery wonder

Breathing deep
and clearing your mind
Feel the spark of life within
Fiery
Molten
Passion blooming
Vibrantly alive
And dancing
Twisting through your spirit
With energetic ecstasy

Breathe in
Breathe out
Draw it up
Draw it in

Resting now,
on the Earth
And in this circle (of women)
(In the hand of the Goddess)

Breathing with her
Standing with her
Knowing her
Deeply

Blessed be.

Body Prayer

I roam
sacred ground
my body is my altar
my temple.

I cast a circle
with my breath
I touch the earth
with my fingers
I answer
to the fire of my spirit.

My blood
pulses in time
with larger rhythms
past, present, future
connected
rooted
breathing.

The reach of my fingers
my ritual
the song of my blood
my blessing
my electric mind
my offering.

Breathing deep
stretching out
opening wide.

My body is my altar
my body is my temple
my living presence on this earth
my prayer.

Thank you.

Pregnant with Myself

Soft belly
no longer bearing children
I am pregnant with myself
ripe with potential,
possibility, power
I incubate my dreams
and give birth to my vision.

I cradle my own body here on sacred ground.
Celebrating all that she has brought forward into this world.
Pausing to honor the patient creativity of my womb,
the pulse of my blood,
and the rhythms of my life.

Thank you
holy one
thank you
sacred space within
thank you
hopeful spirit
thank you
embracing Goddess
of my heart and planet...

Bloodtime

Bloodtime
Moontime
Dreamtime
Darktime
thinking time
resting time
knowing time
hearing time
listening time

openness

flowing
knowing
transforming
becoming
whole...

Bloodtime, Moontime

Bloodtime
moontime
dreamtime
womb time
rest time.

Pause
stop
celebrate
consecrate
honor
breathe
feel...
touch

with potential and promise
sing with the planet
dance with desire
hold your wishes close to your heart
incubate them lovingly

gather up your resources
gather in yourself
cocooning
safe, held and loved
building power
holding power
collecting body wisdom
listening deeply

draw it to you
hold it close

emerge with strength
clarity
purpose
energy
and renewal.

This is a time of powerful medicine if you remember to listen.

Pelvic Cradle

One hand on pelvic cradle
one hand on solid stone
I complete the energetic circle
that brought me into being.

Of this earth
on this earth
from this earth.
My body woven with the mysteries
of time and space.
My life connected
to those around me
human and nonhuman.

Closed eyes blessed by sunshine
body held in stone embrace
mind stilled
shoulders relaxed
heartbeat in my veins
matched to the pulse of Life itself.

She is weaver
and web.

I am weaver
and web
and this great, grand, unimaginable
tapestry of being
is holy and eternal
magnificent and microscopic.

Hand on pelvic cradle
hand on solid stone
energy flow
of cellular connection
unbreakable
in its potency,
everchanging.

Hand on pelvic cradle
hand on solid stone
I draw in the breath of life
draw in my awareness of connection
to the intricate web of incarnation.

Goddess is my name for
that which holds the whole
that which weaves the all
that which knows the story of the ages.

Hand on pelvic cradle
hand on solid stone
I feel the fire in my heart
the red thread in my veins and womb
connects me to women of all times and places
the breath of life in my lungs
the kiss of Earth along my spine...

Womanprayers

excerpted from Earthprayer, Birthprayer, Lifeprayer, Womanprayer

(available from: etsy.com/listing/213185548/earthprayer-birthprayer-lifeprayer)

Medicine Woman

Medicine Woman
She who heals

Reaching out
strong hands
supple wrists
cleansing touch
place your hand in hers
and you will feel it...

Energy
passing from one to another
conduit of grace
and repair.

Restoration

Medicine Woman reminds you
to sleep when you're tired
to eat when you're hungry
to drink when you're thirsty
and to dance
just because.

Medicine Woman
let her bind up your wounds
apply balm to your soul
and hold you
against her shoulder
when you need to cry.

Medicine Woman
Earth healer
she's ready to embrace you.

Yoga Woman

Yoga Woman
she's stretching out
opening her arms to the sun
swooping forward
gathering the moon in her arms
stretching from side to side.

Yoked to divinity
with her steady breath
Yoked to infinity
through the supple movements of her body.

In tree pose, she finds her balance
despite asymmetry
flexible, yielding
strong, and steady
one-legged and whole.

She is centered
she is ever-changing
she throws back her head
and laughs with the Goddess

Expansive core
strong legs
squared shoulders
she carries an ancient body wisdom
linking her to that which has come before
that which will come after
and to the steady pulse of
All That Is.

Yoga woman
Full body cellular activation
Occurring through each cosmic respiration.

Moonpriestess

Moonmaiden
Moonmother
Moonpriestess

She tilts her face to the sky
she opens her arms wide
she draws it down
clean
healing
holy moonlight
enlivening her being
lightening her footsteps
and guiding her path

Moon guide
moon guardian
shining one
sacred spirit
we call upon you
for healing
for wisdom
for inspiration
for guidance

You connect us
in sacred rhythm
to the heartbeat
of the planet
the pull
of the tides
the pulse
of our blood.

We hope
we laugh
we sing
we pray
we dance
by your light
in your rhythm
we drum
in your sacred power

Keeper of ancient wisdom
witness to unfathomable eons
may we be forever
inspired by our connection to you
enlivened by your wisdom
and guided by your truth

Shakti Woman

Shakti woman
coiled within
fiery voice
running snakelike up my spine
bursting free
in the language and poetry
of leaves and stones

Poems gather within me
coiled at the base of my spine
stirred in the cauldron of my belly
cradled by the bones of my hips
waiting until such time
as they spiral upwards
through my chest and throat
and past my waiting lips
speaking words
in patterns I've never heard before
and yet that waited inside me to be born.

Shakti woman
unfurling
speaking through my mouth
caressing the planet with her breath
divine union
oracle
open heart
open throat
sweet
rich
biting
burning
energy of creation

Shakti woman
I honor you
I carry you
looped loosely
like a belt around my hips
shining from my eyes
tasting your words on my tongue
and in my heart.

Prophet Woman

She's been waiting
curled up
knees to chest
head to arms
sleeping
thinking
biding her time
but her eyes have flickered open
she's stretching her arms
unfolding her legs
wriggling into her purpose
until it fits like a glove

She's opened up her heart
and her throat
and her voice comes pouring forth
like a swirling river
her ear is tuned
to the hopesong of the forest
her heart is tuned
to the rhythm of the earth
she feels the Goddess sing through her
alive in her blood
and she steps forth...

She rattles cages
she stirs the pot
she shakes things up
she asks hard questions
she refuses to accept no
and you can't.

She digs deeper
she twists harder
she wonders more
she speaks her truth.

Soon cages bend and open
veils fall away
fires of curiosity are lit
in hopeful breasts
and wisdom no longer belongs to secret places.

The world is reborn
knowing love as the ground of being
and the source of all creation.

and refusing to kill anything
but illusion and despair.

Prophet Woman
she's a warrior
speaking now
her voice is quiet
in this moment
but I hear
the distant thunder
and I feel
the breath of change
against my neck.

Mamapriestess

She who changes
She who expands and contracts
She who stretches her limits
She who digs deep
She who triumphs and fails
Every day
Sometimes both within a single hour
She who tends her own hearth
She who comforts and connects and enfolds
She who opens *wide*
She whose heart cracks open at birth
She who tension bunches her shoulders
And lines her face
She who laughs
She who carries the world
She who sings with her sisters
And circles in ceremony
She who holds precious her daughters and her sons
She who defends and protects
She who opens her heart just a *little* wider
She who trusts
She who tries again
She who gathers to her breast
She who gathers women in ritual
She who hopes
Prays
Fears
She who loves *so deeply*
That it crosses all boundaries
To eternity.

She is Crone

Crone
Wise woman
Sage woman
Grandmother

Her cloak of many colors
Is woven from the threads
Of a million stories
Part of the fiber of her being

Her righteous anger is carried
In the soles of her feet
No longer apologetic
She walks with purpose

Like water upon rock
Time has made its mark
Left its patterns on her body
Carved her away
To her most essential self

Around her waist she gathers
Her girdle of power
She holds her wise blood
Her cells imprinted
With the memories and potential
Of a thousand generations
Children have written upon her body
And she carries it well

These breasts have fed
The world
These shoulders have borne
Heavy burdens
These hips have cradled infants
Have carried children
And danced with friends and lovers

She who changes
She cannot be pinned down
Her multicolored cloak
Shifts its pattern in the breeze
Carrying the voices
And the wisdom of the years

She wraps her cloak of stories around her
Scoops up dreams with wide arms
Tilts her face to the sky
Whispers a blessing on the wind

She picks up her staff of memory
She sings the song of experience
And she takes another step
In the river of time…

Womanrunes in the Red Tent

What are Womanrunes and why use them?

Womanrunes are a unique and powerful divination system that use simple, woman-identified symbols to connect deeply with your own inner wisdom as well as the flow of womanspirit knowledge that surrounds you. Used as a personal oracle, they offer spiritual insight, understanding, and guidance as well as calls to action and discovery. Women who use them are amazed to discover how the symbols and interpretations reach out with *exactly what you need in that moment.* Women's experiences with Womanrunes are powerful, magical, inspirational, potent, and mystical. The wisdom within them can be drawn upon again and again, often uncovering new information, understanding, and truth with each reading.

Herstory

On the Summer Solstice of 1987 after having worked with traditional runes, but sensing "something more" behind them, Shekhinah Mountainwater "fell into a state of enchantment" and in a single day created a 41 symbol woman-identified rune system to be used for divination, self-understanding, guidance, and personal growth.

In 2012, I was reading a back issue of SageWoman magazine from 1988 and stumbled across an article about Womanrunes. I instantly fell in love with them. They issued a powerful call to me. I scoured the internet for more information, where I eventually found a handout and pronunciation guide on an old website. I purchased Shekhinah's classic book of women's spirituality, Ariadne's Thread, and began making Womanrunes sets at women's spirituality retreats with my friends. After working with the symbols for some time, I began to sense more detailed interpretations for them. I began choosing one each day, going to a sacred place in the woods with it and discovering what it had to tell me. Over the course of 18 months, this powerful practice developed in a complete guidebook to interpreting and using Womanrunes.

How to Use

The simplest and most common use for Womanrunes is to draw a card daily or when you feel an intuitive need for guidance. Draw the card and *feel* into it. What is it sharing with you? Read the companion interpretation and let it soak in. Many women are amazed by how these symbols speak to something deep within them. You may have the experience of feeling *heard and answered* when you choose a card and read its interpretation. Womanrunes provide a pathway to your own "truth-sense." They open you up to your own internal guidance or to messages and inspiration from the Goddess, the Earth, or your spiritual guides. Womanrunes may also be used to do guidance readings for friends or clients. Messages from Womanrunes are not prescriptive or directive, instead they serve as a rich conduit to exactly what you need to hear and receive in that moment.

Many women have found that Womanrunes make an excellent addition to their Red Tent work. For Red Tent Circles with others, the Womanrunes book and cards can be available in a divination, guidance, or inspiration corner. Create a quiet, nurturing nook in your Red Tent space where the women can sit with the cards, drop into their own heartspace, and receive the message they need.

There are many additional uses for Womanrunes, including creating bindrunes, runewriting, runespells. Many women also find them satisfying to draw or carve onto art, calendars, sculptures and more. Used in this way, the Womanrunes can attract their messages deeply into your life or can serve as potent declarations of intention.

Why Such Simple Images?

Many divination and oracle systems include beautiful artwork on the cards. Womanrunes are simple symbols and are, in fact, a type of symbol "writing" that speaks to a deep part of the soul. The clean focus and simplicity of the Womanrunes symbols evoke rich messages and soul guidance in their own special way that differs from the image-rich paintings of other systems. They are also very easy to use directly yourself—including them in your own art, drawing or etching them onto objects, and thereby writing them into your consciousness in a *living* manner. Used as a dynamic, hands-on, participatory system, Womanrunes become part of your own *language* of the Divine, the Goddess, your inner wisdom, and womanspirit truths.

2: The Crescent Moon.

Rune of Divination.
Ritual.
Door to Unconscious.

Digging Deeper

There are many innovative ways to use Womanrunes in the Red Tent. One of the most powerful aspects of this system is that Womanrunes become *part of your womanspirit language*. They are easily reproducible without any specific talent with art required. This is a divination system you can *use* in so many ways. Womanrunes are not static, they are a dynamic, living, evolving, invested process. Womanrunes become alive for you and you will discover they are right there to learn from and engage with in many ways every day.

When you work with Womanrunes with other women in the Red Tent it creates a sense of investment and brings you into deeper relationship with the runes, with yourself, and with the guidance around you.

Using Womanrunes for Womanspirit Guidance:

- Have the Womanrunes deck and book available in a divination or intuition corner. This nook should be a reflective space for inner guidance.

- Lay out the cards and book on a table close to the entrance of the red tent space. As women enter, they can draw a card to receive a personal check-in with their deep selves.

- As the circle begins, the cards may be passed around the circle as a basic guidance or intuition check or as a centering process. Women may share their reflections or observations or journal about the message.

- Likewise, Womanrunes may be used to "check-out" once the circle is drawing to a close. Before singing your final song or doing your closing reading, each woman can draw a card and read the interpretation as her message or guidance for her return home.

- If you included meditations, guided visualizations, or discussion prompts in your circle, Womanrunes may be used before or after journaling about these experiences.

- A free starter guide to using Womanrunes is available from brigidsgrove.com. You may print these handouts and use them to get started in exploring Womanrunes together.

Using Womanrunes on Red Tent Projects:

- Make prayer flags—either drawing on the symbols using permanent markers or stitching or embroidering them on. Two possible methods:
    - Each woman may make complete mini set of flags. These may then be flown, by choice or chance, on a dowel in the garden, on a front porch, or from a house plant. Fold the top of the flag down about 1/2 inch and stitch across to leave an opening for a dowel or other hanger. You may wish to hem along a long strip of fabric first and then cut off small sections, rather than hemming each flag individually. All other edges can be left unstitched.
    - Make single flags with certain runes (either intentionally chosen or intuitively chosen).

- Make personal sets of Womanrunes for use at home using any of the following methods:
    - Wood (carve, burn, or draw)
    - Pebble, river stone, or beach stone (consciously collected)
    - Polymer clay
    - Pottery clay
    - Air dry clay
    - Glass pebbles
    - Paper or card
    - Printable set available from brigidsgrove.com. These may be colored and cut out then glued on to stones or mounted on cards)

- Make goddess greeting cards with written greetings, blessings, or wishes

- Create runespells by combining symbols. For example, willpower.

- Write your name or a word of power using the pronunciation guide handout in the book or the free starter kit.

Willpower

- Create a pocket totem or a reminder stone with polymer clay or pottery clay. On this totem, you can include the Womanrunes you'd like to attract, manifest, or embody. Or, you can write your name or other word. You may also intuitively select which symbols to include.

- Create the Womanrunes symbols using other mediums (I'm fond of using polished gemstones and forming the symbols out of the gems and then taking a photo of them).

- Make photo collages using your Womanrunes reading and include the inspiration, lessons, messages you've gained from them.

- Write, carve, or paint Womanrunes on:
    - drum
    - bed sheet
    - rattle
    - candle
    - poster or sign
    - goddess figurine
    - book or journal
    - clothing (embroider)
    - sculpture

- Draw Womanrunes on your body—I learned from one of my Womanrunes Immersion students to use liquid eyeliner to ink the symbol of the day (drawn in the morning as a centering or guidance practice) on the inside of the wrist or ankle. This symbol then serves as a mindfulness or guidance cue throughout day. The process of inking the symbols on your skin is a beautifully embodied, physical practice that makes a visceral connection to Womanrunes. You are literally drawing them into you.

- Paint Womanrunes on yourself or in group with other women using body paint—this can be done for empowerment, affirmation, encouragement, healing, blessing, or fun.

- As the year draws to a close, create Calamoondalas for the upcoming year together (see pages 66-71).

Womanrunes book and card sets are available from brigidsgrove.etsy.com. Molly offers a 41 Day Womanrunes Immersion twice a year and a Divination Practicum and workshop training in October.

Note: Wholesale books are available for purchase if you are a Red Tent facilitator who wants to buy multiple copies for members of your circle as you work on your projects. Contact us at brigidsgrove@gmail.com to request a wholesale order.

Quotes for Discussion and Exploration

Some women find it helpful to use these quotes as prompts for sparking communal discussion in a Red Tent Circle and for contextualizing our personal experiences against the larger cultural backdrop. Other facilitators may use them as journaling or art prompts.

> "Women's mysteries, the blood mysteries of the body, are not the same as the physical realities of menstruation, lactation, pregnancy, and menopause; for physiology to become mystery, a mystical affiliation must be made between a woman and the archetypal feminine...
>
> Under patriarchy, this connection has been suppressed; there are no words or rituals that celebrate the connection between a woman's physiological initiations and spiritual meaning."
>
> —Jean Shinoda Bolen, Crossing to Avalon

> "Blood Mysteries recall the immense power of the bleeding woman. Power enough to share in great nourishing give-aways. Give-away from woman womb to earth womb, give-away from mother to matrix, give-away of nourisher to nourisher...bleeding freely, we know ourselves as women, as nourishers of life..."
>
> –Susan Weed

> "What you do on the first day of your cycle radically affects your health and happiness for the next 30 (or so) days. It impacts your relationships, creativity, energy, spiritual connectedness, and self-confidence, just to name a few things..."
>
> Your period is a vehicle for greater compassion in the world at large.
> Your period is a universal language.
> Yet, it's one of the least understood by women today.
> It's one of the topics that is least talked about in our modern culture...
>
> –Pleasurable Periods

> "Human connections are deeply nurtured in the field of shared story."
>
> –Jean Houston

"It is now time for all women of the colorful mind, who are aware of the cycles of night and day and the dance of the moon in her tides, to arise."

—Dhyani Ywahoo (in Open Mind, 11/22)

"Woman-to-woman help through the rites of passage that are important in every birth has significance not only for the individuals directly involved, but for the whole community. The task in which the women are engaged is political. It forms the warp and weft of society."

—Sheila Kitzinger (Rediscovering Birth)

"I love and respect birth. The body is a temple, it creates its own rites, its own prayers...all we must do is listen. With the labor and birth of my daughter I went so deep down, so far into the underworld that I had to crawl my way out. I did this only by surrendering. I did this by trusting the goddess in my bones. She moved through me and has left her power in me."

—Lea B., Fairfax, CA via (Mama Birth)

"Our rites of passage create and sustain culture, our inner culture and the outer culture. The current dominant culture is one of blame and victimhood and unconscious rites of passage reinforce this, within and without. Conscious rites of passage in a likeminded group of folk, creates and reinforces a culture of self responsibility and inner power. It is said that if a young woman does not experience an empowering menarche, then she doesn't start womanhood with a relationship with the empowered feminine."

—JHC

*"For months I just looked at you
I wondered about all the mothers before me
if they looked at their babies the way I looked at you.
In an instant I knew what moved humankind
from continent to continent
Against all odds."*

—Michelle Singer (in We'Moon 2011 datebook)

> "I believe that these circles of women around us weave invisible nets of love that carry us when we're weak and sing with us when we're strong."
>
> —SARK, Succulent Wild Woman

> "There is a wild tiger in every woman's heart. Its hot and holy breath quietly, relentlessly feeding her."
>
> – Chameli Ardagh

> "Nothing will change as long as women say nothing."
>
> —Cynthia Blynn

> "We are the torchbearers of truth, the tellers of tales of beautiful birth, the weavers of courageous empowering visions to set before the women and families we serve. Our stories must be told often, until they become more compelling and convincing than the horrible [...] myths people hear all around them."
>
> —Judy Edmunds

> "Honouring our menstrual cycle reminds us how sacred we are."
>
> —Jane Hardwicke Collings, Becoming A Woman

> "Childbearing is a form of power, one of the greatest powers in the world, and menstruation is a sign of that power."
>
> —Valerie Tarico

> "We are born into blood and with blood."
>
> -Chandra Alexandre, at The Conference on Earth-Based Spiritualities & Gender

"The psyches and souls of women have their own cycles and seasons of doing and solitude, running and staying, being involved and being removed, questing and resting, creating and incubating, being of the world and returning to the soul-place...

In order to converse with the wild feminine, a woman must temporarily leave the world and inhabit a state of aloneness in the oldest sense of the word. Long ago the word alone was treated as two words, all one. To be all one, meant to be wholly one, to be in oneness, either essentially or temporarily. That is precisely the goal of solitude, to be all one. It is the cure for the frazzled state so common to modern women..."

--Clarissa Pinkola Estés, Women Who Run with the Wolves

Womanspirit Wisdom for Red Tent Circles: Moon Time

One of my favorite books to have available on the resource table of our local Red Tent Circle is *Moon Time*, by Lucy Pearce (thehappywomb.com). Sharing womanspirit wisdom quotes at the beginning of a Red Tent Circle is one way to stimulate discussion in the circle. Here are some quotes from *Moon Time* that can serve as provocative launching points for a sharing circle in the Red Tent:

> *"It is my guess that no one ever initiated you into the path of womanhood. Instead, just like me, you were left to find out by yourself. Little by little you pieced a working understanding of your body and soul together. But still you have gaps."*
>
> **Questions for circle:** Were you initiated into the "path of womanhood"? What gaps do you feel?

> *"You yearn for a greater knowledge of your woman's body, a comprehensive understanding of who you are, why you are that way. Perhaps you have searched long and hard, seeking advice from your mother, sister, aunts and friends, tired of suffering and struggling alone. You may have visited doctors, healers or therapists, but still you feel at sea and your woman's body is a mystery to you. Or maybe you have never given your cycles a second thought ... until now."*
>
> **Questions for circle:** What do you feel like you need to know about your body? What mysteries are you uncovering?

> *"Through knowledge we gain power over our lives. With options we have possibility. With acceptance we find a new freedom.*
> *Menstruation matters."*
>
> **Question for circle:** How does menstruation matter?

Additional information from *Moon Time* about *why* menstruation matters on a physical, emotional, and relational level:

> *We start bleeding earlier today than ever before, with girls' first periods occurring at 12.8 years old now, compared with 14.5 years at the beginning of the last century. Coupled with lower breastfeeding rates, better nutrition and fewer pregnancies, women now menstruate more in their adult lives than at any time in our history.*
>
> *From the age of 12 to 51, unless you are pregnant or on the pill, every single day of your life as a woman is situated somewhere on the menstrual cycle. Whether ovulating or bleeding, struggling with PMS or conception, our bodies, our energy levels, our sense of self, even our abilities are constantly shifting each and every day. And yet nobody talks about it...*

This book was helpful to me personally in acknowledging myself as a cyclical being and that these influences are physical and *real*:

> Each month our bodies go through a series of changes, many of which we may be unconscious of. These include: shifts in levels of hormones, vitamins and minerals, vaginal temperature and secretions, the structure of the womb lining and cervix, body weight, water retention, heart rate, breast size and texture, attention span, pain threshold . . .
>
> The changes are biological. Measurable. They are most definitely not 'all in your head' as many would have us believe. This is why it is so crucial to honour these changes by adapting our lives to them as much as possible.
>
> **We cannot just will these changes not to happen as they are an integral part of our fertility.**

"There is no shame in tears. There is a need for anger. Blood will flow. Speak your truth. Follow your intuition. Nurture your body. But above all ... Let yourself rest."

Questions for circle: Do you allow yourself anger and tears? Do you feel shame? How do you speak your truth? How do you give yourself time to rest?

"There is little understanding and allowance for the realities of being a cycling woman— let alone celebration."

Questions for circle: What allowances do you make for yourself as a cycling woman? Are you able to celebrate the experience?

> "Moontime opens up our intuition.
> By allowing ourselves to honour this time,
> we can eliminate premenstrual tendencies...
> Moontime is a sacred passage leading
> to a greater awareness of self."
> –Veronika Robinson, Cycle to the Moon (p. 142)

Moon Time is available from Lucy's website: thehappywomb.com/

Womenergy

The day before my grandma died, my dad came over and said he'd coined a new word and that I could have it: **Womenergy.** I dozed off during my daughter's nap and when I woke up the word was in my head and so were a chorus of other words. I channeled a bit of my inner Alice Walker and wrote:

Womenergy

Often felt when giving birth. Also felt at mother blessings and circling with women in ceremony and rituals. Involved in the fabric of creation and breath of life. Drawn upon when nursing babies and toting toddlers. Known also as womanpower, closely related to womanspirit and the hearing of one's "sacred roar." That which is wild, fierce. Embedded and embodied, it may also be that which has been denied and suppressed and yet waits below her surface, its hot, holy breath igniting her. Experienced as the "invisible nets of love" that surround us, womenergy makes meals for postpartum women, hugs you when you cry, smiles in solidarity at melting down toddlers. It is the force that rises in the night to take care of sick children, that which holds hands with the dying, and stretches out arms to the grieving. It sits with laboring women, nurses the sick, heals the wounded, and nurtures the young. It dances in the moonlight. Womenergy is that which holds the space, that which bears witness, that which hears and sees one another into speech, into being, into personal power. Called upon when digging deep, trying again, and rising up. That which cannot be silenced. The heart and soul of connection. The small voice within that says, *"maybe I can, I think I can, I know I can. I AM doing it. Look what I did!"* Creates art, weaves words, births babies, gathers people. Thinks in circles, webs, and patterns rather than in lines and angles. Felt as action, resistance, creation, struggle, power, and inherent wisdom.

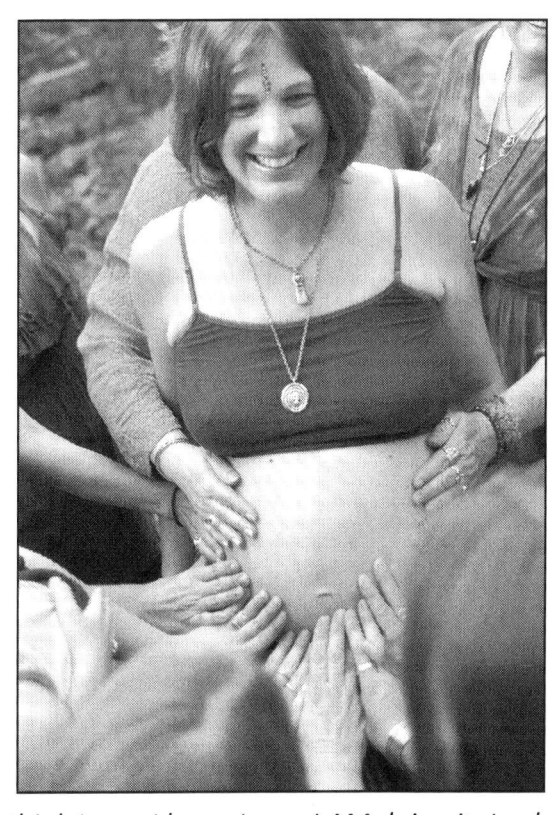

Womenergy moved humanity across continents, birthed civilization, invented agriculture, conceived of art and writing, pottery, sculpture, and drumming, painted cave walls, raised sacred stones and built Goddess temples. It rises anew during ritual, sacred song, and drumming together. It says *She Is Here. I Am Here. You Are Here* and *We Can Do This*. It speaks through women's hands, bodies, and heartsongs. Felt in hope, in tears, in blood, and in triumph.

Womenergy is the chain of the generations, the "red thread" that binds us womb to womb across time and space to the women who have come before and those who will come after. Spinning stories, memories, and bodies, it is that force which unfolds the body of humanity from single cells, to spiraled souls, and pushes them forth into the waiting world.

Used in a sentence:

"I'm headed to the women's circle tonight. I could really use the womenergy."

"I felt like I couldn't keep going, but then my womenergy rose up and I did it anyway."

"Feel the womenergy in this room!"

"She said she didn't think she could give birth after all, but then she tapped into her womenergy and kept going."

"I hope my friends have a mother blessing for me, I need to be reminded of the womenergy that surrounds me as I get ready to have this baby."

Feel it…
Listen to it…
Know it…

In the air, in her touch, in your soul.

Rising
Potent
Embodied
Yours…

Resources & References

Facebook
- Occupy Menstruation
- Red Tents in every neighborhood
- Women Rise Up with ALisa Starkweather
- The Way of the Happy Woman
- Red Tent Movie: "Things We Don't Talk About"
- Red Tent Dreaming
- The Happy Womb
- Red Tent Festival
- Red Tent Health Centre – for women & their families
- Operation: Red Tent
- Red Tent Circle Halifax
- Red Tent Temple of Charleston
- Crimson Movement
- Moontime Rising
- Denver Red Tent Collective
- Moon Mysteries
- Her Blood Is Gold: Awakening to the Wisdom of Menstruation
- Red Tent Manchester
- Red Web Foundation

Books
- Becoming Peers by DeAnna Lam
- The Goddess Path: Myths, Invocations, & Rituals by Patricia Monaghan
- Honoring Menstruation by Lara Owen
- Keep Simple Ceremonies by Diane Eiker
- Mandala by Judith Cornell
- Menarche by Rachael Hertogs
- Moon Mysteries by Nao Sims and Nikiah Seeds
- Moon Time by Lucy Pearce
- Reaching for the Moon by Lucy Pearce
- Red Moon by Miranda Gray
- Sacred Circles by Robin Deen Carnes and Sally Craig
- SoulCollage by Seena B. Frost
- The Thundering Years: Rituals and Sacred Wisdom for Teens by Julie Tallard Johnson
- The Woman's Retreat Book by Jennifer Louden
- Women's Rites of Passage by Hermitra Crecraft
- Women Who Run with the Wolves by Clarissa Pinkola Estes

Websites
- deannalam.com/
- thehappywomb.com/
- alisastarkweather.com/
- moontimes.co.uk/
- redtentmovie.com/red-tent-tv.html

How to Make a Calamoondala

By Molly Remer

brigidsgrove.com

Supplies needed:
- 12 x 18 piece of black paper (construction paper or charcoal paper)
- White colored pencil (I use Prismacolor colored pencils)
- Plate, mug, and coin (a quarter or similar size) or other circular objects to draw around
- Full and new moon dates for the year (available online use the We'Moon calendar, wemoon.ws)
- Optional: Womanrunes deck or other oracle cards (Womanrunes available here: brigidsgrove.etsy.com)

Note: This is a very organic, intuitive, and free-flowing process. Honor your own instincts. The suggestions above are only suggestions, you can use colored paper, colored pencils, smaller or larger paper, include all moon phases, etc. I find it helpful to have six white pencils with sharp points ready to go so I can quickly switch to a fresh pencil when the point dulls (this happens very rapidly with soft colored pencils). Either that or keep a pencil sharpener very handy!

I have been creating a full moon "Calamoondala" at the start of each new year for the last four years. I began by calling it a Calamandala, meaning a calendar in a round, patterned design like a mandala. Since, I use mine as a means of dating the full moons for a year, I realized that "Calamoondala" is an even better name! A Calamoondala is a circular calendar tracking the full moons over the course of a year using a mandala-type design. I use mine to identify new moons as well and others may choose to include waning moons. The Calamoondala can also include an annual oracle element by drawing oracle cards from a deck like Womanrunes for each moon and including their symbols in your design.

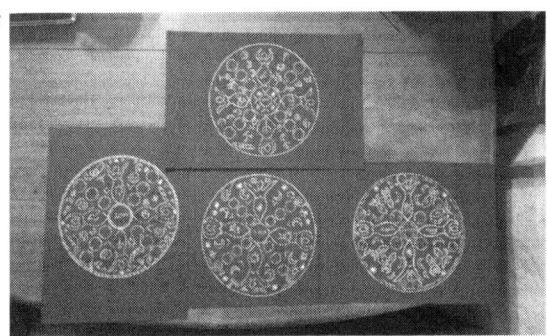

Begin by using your white pencil to trace a large circle in the center of your black paper.

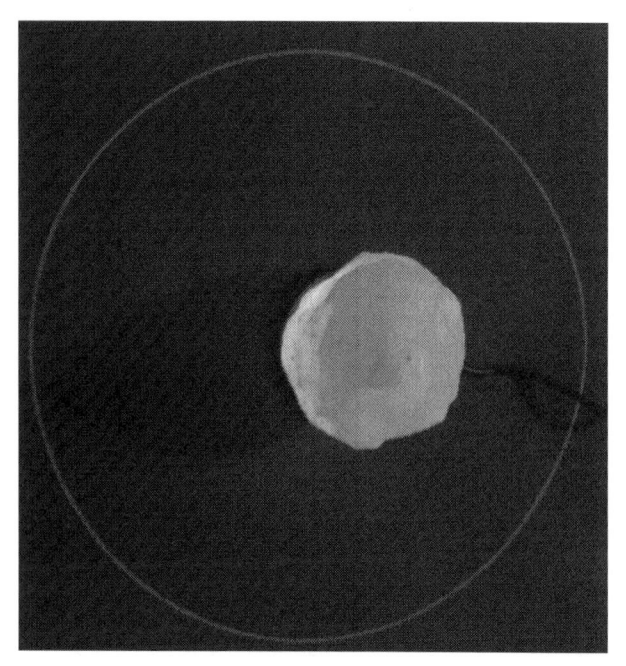

Trace another circle in the center using the rim of a mug or small saucer. And, if you feel like it, use a quarter to trace still another circle in the center of that one!

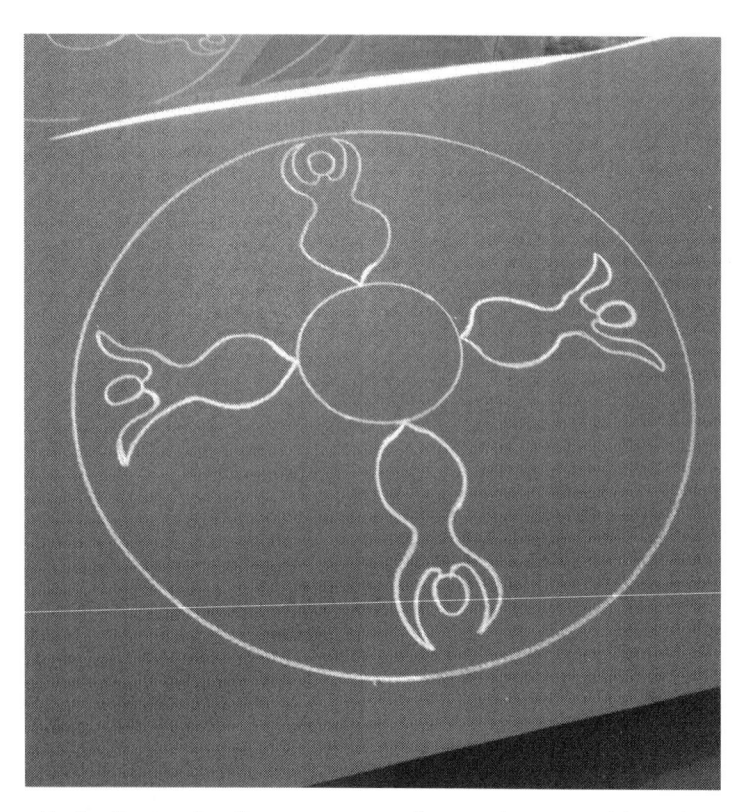

To indicate the four seasons, draw a large goddess (or other personally meaningful symbol) in each quarter of your big circle.

Then, trace around your coin to indicate each full moon in the year, four moons per quarter. In 2015, July has two full moons, so you can include a circle for the 13th moon or for symmetry's sake include both July dates on one circle.

Add dates to each moon. I put the month at the top and the day at the bottom of each moon (using small numbers so as not to be distracting) and work outward from the center.

Restoring Women to Ceremony: The Red Tent Resource Kit

Add four crescent moons and the dates of each new moon to each quadrant of your design (for 2015, I lined them up on the right side of each full moon and included my Womanrunes reading for each month on the left side of each moon).

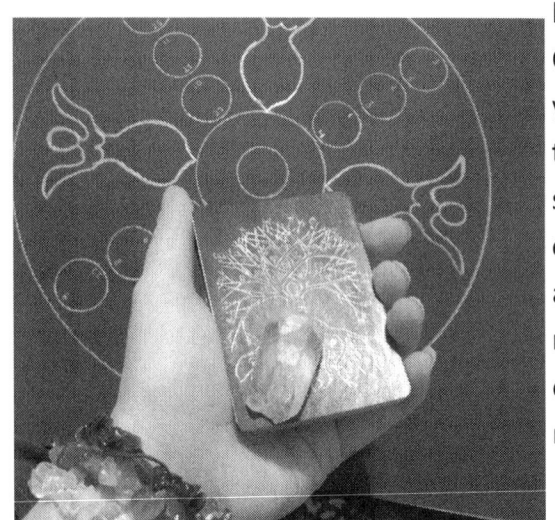

If you would like to include an annual oracle as an aspect of your Calamoondala, center yourself with your Womanrunes deck in your hands. Take some deep breaths, close your eyes, and feel into the cards with your intuition. Draw one card for each of the four seasons and draw those symbols on the four goddess figures. These are your broad themes as you move through the year. Add the cards back to the deck and reshuffle.

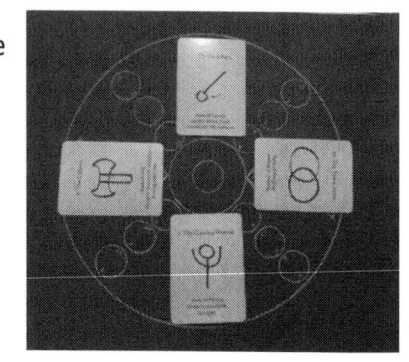

Draw one card for each moon of the year. Add the Womanrunes (or other symbol) to your Calamoondala.

These represent your messages, themes, or focus for each moon cycle.

Include any other symbols or design elements you would like and put the year in the center!

Another note: There is no perfect. There is no "right way." I drew my 2013 Calamoondala with a toddler sitting on my back! My 2015 calamoondala was drawn in my bed on an uneven surface, with a baby nursing held in one arm while I traced around my quarter with my free hand. For part of the time, my four year old drew on her own piece of paper in bed with me, while alternately getting too close to my own drawing and wrinkling the edges. I don't use a compass, just "eyeball it" and my eyeballs sometimes misjudge, so it isn't perfectly symmetrical, nor are my lines even and the goddesses and my symbols are far from smooth or perfect. The Calamoondala creation process is like a metaphor for life. It IS life. The secret is to just do it!

Restoring Women to Ceremony: The Red Tent Resource Kit

About the author:

Molly has been gathering the women to circle, sing, celebrate, and share since 2008. She plans and facilitates women's circles, seasonal retreats and rituals, mother-daughter circles, family ceremonies, and red tent circles in rural Missouri. She is an ordained priestess who holds MSW and M.Div degrees and she is currently writing her dissertation about contemporary priestessing in the U.S. Molly's roots are in birth work and in domestic violence activism. She has worked with groups of women since 1996 and teaches college courses in group dynamics and human services.

Molly has maintained her Talk Birth blog (talkbirth.me) since 2007 and writes about thealogy, nature, practical priestessing, and the goddess at her Woodspriestess blog (goddesspriestess.com).

About Brigid's Grove:

Molly and Mark co-create original birth art jewelry, figurines, goddess pendants, and ceremony kits at brigidsgrove.com. They publish *Womanrunes: a guide to their use and interpretation* and an accompanying oracle deck, based on the work of Shekhinah Mountainwater.

Brigid's Grove integrates Molly's priestess work with our family's shared interests in ceremony, art, gemstones, metalwork, nature, and intentional, creative living.

Brigid is the Irish triple goddess of smithcraft, poetry, and midwifery. She is also a Christian saint associated with midwives, birthing mothers, and infants.

Continue your work with us:

Our ceremony kits, art, and jewelry are available from brigidsgrove.etsy.com. We have a free Creative Ceremony Academy group on Facebook (facebook.com/groups/722938817814977) and a companion resource page on our website: brigidsgrove.com/creative-ceremony-academy/.

Molly teaches a detailed, resource-full, immersive Red Tent Initiation course online each spring and fall. Check the site above for upcoming dates. This course is both a powerful, personal experience *and* a training in facilitating transformative women's circles.

Printed in Great Britain
by Amazon.co.uk, Ltd.,
Marston Gate.